SCHOLASTIC

READ & RESPOND

Bringing the best books to life in the classroom

Activities based on

Varjak Paw

By SF Said

Recommended system requirements:
Windows: XP (Service Pack 3), Vista (Service Pack 2), Windows 7 or Windows 8 with 2.33GHz processor
Mac: OS 10.6 to 10.8 with Intel Core™ Duo processor
1GB RAM (recommended)
1024 x 768 Screen resolution
CD-ROM drive (24x speed recommended)
Adobe Reader (version 9 recommended for Mac users)
Broadband internet connections (for installation and updates)

For all technical support queries (including no CD drive), please phone Scholastic Customer Services on 0845 6039091.

Designed using Adobe Indesign
Scholastic Education, an imprint of Scholastic Ltd
Book End, Range Road, Witney, Oxfordshire, OX29 0YD
Registered office: Westfield Road, Southam, Warwickshire CV47 0RA

Printed and bound by Ashford Colour Press
© 2017 Scholastic Ltd
1 2 3 4 5 6 7 8 9   7 8 9 0 1 2 3 4 5 6

British Library Cataloguing-in-Publication Data
A catalogue record for this book is available from the British Library.
ISBN 978-1407-16069-6

Due to the nature of the web, we cannot guarantee the content or links of any site mentioned. We strongly recommend that teachers check websites before using them in the classroom.

Author Sally Burt and Debbie Ridgard
Editorial team Rachel Morgan, Jenny Wilcox, Becky Breuer and Jennie Clifford
Series designer Neil Salt
Designer Anna Oliwa
Illustrator Jan Smith/Beehive Illustration
Digital development Hannah Barnett, Phil Crothers and MWA Technologies Private Ltd

Acknowledgements
The publishers gratefully acknowledge permission to reproduce the following copyright material:
Penguin Random House UK for the use of the cover and extract text from *Varjak Paw* written by S.F. Said, first published in Great Britain by David Fickling Books, (when an imprint of Random House Children's Publishers UK A Random House Group Company) Copyright © S.F. Said, 2003. Illustrations copyright © Dave McKean, 2003. (2014, Corgi Books)

Every effort has been made to trace copyright holders for the works reproduced in this book, and the publishers apologise for any inadvertent omissions.

CONTENTS

INTRODUCTION

Read & Respond provides teaching ideas related to a specific children's book. The series focuses on best-loved books and brings you ways to use them to engage your class and enthuse them about reading.

The book is divided into different sections:

- **About the book and author:** gives you some background information about the book and the author.

- **Guided reading:** breaks the book down into sections and gives notes for using it with guided reading groups. A bookmark has been provided on page 12 containing comprehension questions. The children can be directed to refer to these as they read.

- **Shared reading:** provides extracts from the children's books with associated notes for focused work. There is also one non-fiction extract that relates to the children's book.

- **Grammar, punctuation & spelling:** provides word-level work related to the children's book so you can teach grammar, punctuation and spelling in context.

- **Plot, character & setting:** contains activity ideas focused on the plot, characters and the setting of the story.

- **Talk about it:** has speaking and listening activities related to the children's book. These activities may be based directly on the children's book or be broadly based on the themes and concepts of the story.

- **Get writing:** provides writing activities related to the children's book. These activities may be based directly on the children's book or be broadly based on the themes and concepts of the story.

- **Assessment:** contains short activities that will help you assess whether the children have understood concepts and curriculum objectives. They are designed to be informal activities to feed into your planning.

The activities follow the same format:

- **Objective:** the objective for the lesson. It will be based upon a curriculum objective, but will often be more specific to the focus being covered.

- **What you need:** a list of resources you need to teach the lesson, including digital resources (printable pages, interactive activities and media resources, see page 5).

- **What to do:** the activity notes.

- **Differentiation:** this is provided where specific and useful differentiation advice can be given to support and/or extend the learning in the activity. Differentiation by providing additional adult support has not been included as this will be at a teacher's discretion based upon specific children's needs and ability, as well as the availability of support.

The activities are numbered for reference within each section and should move through the text sequentially – so you can use the lesson while you are reading the book. Once you have read the book, most of the activities can be used in any order you wish.

Below are brief guidance notes for using the CD-ROM. For more detailed information, please click on the '?' button in the top right-hand corner of the screen.

The program contains the following:

- the extract pages from the book
- all of the photocopiable pages from the book
- additional printable pages
- interactive on-screen activities
- media resources.

Getting started

Put the CD-ROM into your CD-ROM drive. If you do not have a CD-ROM drive, phone Scholastic Customer Services on 0845 6039091.

- For Windows users, the install wizard should autorun, if it fails to do so then navigate to your CD-ROM drive. Then follow the installation process.
- For Mac users, copy the disk image file to your hard drive. After it has finished copying double click it to mount the disk image. Navigate to the mounted disk image and run the installer. After installation the disk image can be unmounted and the DMG can be deleted from the hard drive.
- To install on a network, see the ReadMe file located on the CD-ROM (navigate to your drive).

To complete the installation of the program you need to open the program and click 'Update' in the pop-up. Please note – this CD-ROM is web-enabled and the content will be downloaded from the internet to your hard drive to populate the CD-ROM with the relevant resources. This only needs to be done on first use, after this you will be able to use the CD-ROM without an internet connection. If at any point any content is updated, you will receive another pop-up upon start up when there is an internet connection.

Main menu

The main menu is the first screen that appears. Here you can access: terms and conditions, registration links, how to use the CD-ROM and credits. To access a specific book click on the relevant button (note only titles installed will be available). You can filter by the drop-down lists if you wish. You can search all resources by clicking 'Search' in the bottom left-hand corner. You can also log in and access favourites that you have bookmarked.

Resources

By clicking on a book on the Main menu, you are taken to the resources for that title. The resources are: Media, Interactives, Extracts and Printables. Select the category and then launch a resource by clicking the play button.

Teacher settings

In the top right-hand corner of the screen is a small 'T' icon. This is the teacher settings area. It is password protected, the password is: login. This area will allow you to choose the print quality settings for interactive activities ('Default' or 'Best') and also allow you to check for updates to the program or re-download all content to the disk via 'Refresh all content'. You can also set up user logins so that you can save and access favourites. Once a user is set up, they can enter by clicking the login link underneath the 'T' and '?' buttons.

Search

You can access an all resources search by clicking the search button on the bottom left of the Main menu. You can search for activities by type (using the drop-down filter) or by keyword by typing into the box. You can then assign resources to your favourites area or launch them directly from the search area.

CURRICULUM LINKS

Section	Activity	Curriculum objectives
Guided reading		Comprehension: To maintain positive attitudes to reading and understanding of what they read.
Shared reading	1	Comprehension: To identify how language contributes to meaning.
	2	Comprehension: To identify how structure and presentation contribute to meaning.
	3	Comprehension: To identify how language and structure contribute to meaning.
	4	Comprehension: To maintain positive attitudes to reading and understanding of what they read by discussing non-fiction.
Grammar, punctuation & spelling	1	Composition: To use relative clauses beginning with 'who', 'which', 'where', 'when', 'whose', 'that' or with an implied relative pronoun.
	2	Composition: To use dashes to indicate parenthesis.
	3	Composition: To use a colon to introduce a list.
	4	Transcription: To use prefixes and understand the guidelines for adding them.
	5	Composition: To use devices to build cohesion.
	6	Transcription: To distinguish between homophones and other words which are often confused.
Plot, character & setting	1	Composition: To describe a setting.
	2	Composition: To consider how authors develop characters.
	3	Spoken language: To participate in performances.
	4	Comprehension: To predict what might happen from details stated and implied.
	5	Comprehension: To summarise the main ideas drawn from more than one paragraph, identifying key details that support the main ideas.
	6	Comprehension: To identify and discuss conventions in writing.
	7	Comprehension: To explain and discuss their understanding of what they have read.
	8	Comprehension: To identify and discuss conventions in writing.

Section	Activity	Curriculum objectives
Talk about it	1	Spoken language: To gain, maintain and monitor the interest of the listener.
	2	Spoken language: To use relevant strategies to build their vocabulary.
	3	Spoken language: To participate actively in collaborative conversations.
	4	Spoken language: To participate in discussions and debates.
	5	Spoken language: To participate in role play.
	6	Spoken language: To participate in presentations.
Get writing	1	Composition: To use commas to clarify meaning or avoid ambiguity in writing.
	2	Composition: To plan their writing by discussing writing similar to that which they are planning to write to understand and learn from its structure; to use devices to build cohesion.
	3	Composition: To select appropriate grammar and vocabulary to enhance meaning.
	4	Composition: To use organisational and presentational devices to structure text.
	5	Composition: To recognise structures that are appropriate for formal speech.
	6	Composition: To describe settings, characters and atmosphere, integrating dialogue.
Assessment	1	Comprehension: To understand what they read.
	2	Spoken language: To select and use appropriate registers for effective communication.
	3	Transcription: To use suffixes.
	4	Composition: To identify the audience for and purpose of the writing, selecting the appropriate form.
	5	Composition: To use expanded noun phrases to convey information.
	6	Composition: To evaluate and edit their own writing.

VARJAK PAW

About the book

Varjak Paw, a pure-bred Mesopotamian Blue kitten, who lives a pampered life with his 'noble' cat family in the Contessa's house, is teased by his family about his amber eyes. What is more, Varjak thinks about things true 'Blues' shouldn't, like hunting or venturing Outside! Varjak loves listening to the Elder Paw's tales of Jalal – their famous ancestor, a mighty warrior, hunter and adventurer. Varjak's sheltered existence is suddenly shattered by the arrival of a large gentleman accompanied by two, sleek and sinister black cats. When Varjak sees something being carried away by men, he knows something is wrong but only his grandfather, the Elder Paw, has faith in him. Varjak has to rescue his family by doing the unthinkable. He has to leave the house on the hill and venture Outside in search of a dog and salvation for his family. To guide him, Varjak has only the tales of his ancestor Jalal, and his sketchy knowledge of the Way – an ancient form of cat martial arts passed down by Jalal through generations of Paws. In the city, Varjak learns to survive on his quest to save his family with the help of the Seven Skills Jalal teaches him in his dreams and some unexpected new friends.

This beautifully written, fantasy novel for young readers is full of action, adventure and intrigue. Readers will find themselves caught up in the mysterious Way and riveted by Varjak's determination to survive against all odds.

About the author

SF Said was born in Beirut, Lebanon in 1967 and moved to London at the age of two. After school, he graduated from Cambridge University and worked as a speechwriter for the Crown Prince of Jordan's office in London for six years. While working in journalism and film, he began writing Varjak Paw – his first novel. It was finally published in 2003 after 17 drafts. He is an award-winning author of children's books, a literary judge, reviewer, journalist and popular speaker with adults and children. He has his own web page and author blog where he shares his enthusiasm for literature.

About the illustrator

Dave McKean, born December 1963, is a well-known British illustrator, photographer, artist, musician and film-maker. He has worked with other famous authors, scientists, theatre directors, film producers, TV writers and even chefs to produce award-winning books, films, plays and TV shows.

Key facts

Varjak Paw

Author: SF Said

Illustrator: Dave McKean

First published: 2003 by David Fickling Books, then part of the Random House Group

Awards: Gateshead Children's Book of the Year, West Sussex Children's Book Award, Stockton Children's Book of the Year, Nestlé Smarties Book Prize (Gold Medal)

Did you know? *Varjak Paw* has been adapted for the theatre and performed as an opera. It is also due to be released as an animated family feature film. It has been translated into 12 languages and has reached sales of over 270 000. The sequel, *The Outlaw Varjak Paw*, is the next award-winning title in the series.

Paws for thought

Before reading, investigate the book's cover and ask for predictions on the storyline. Children should easily infer the main character is a cat named Varjak Paw. Scan the cover and preliminary pages for further information, and discuss question 1 on the bookmark (fantasy, adventure), using clues such as 'This cat must learn to fight' on the front cover, reviews and the blurb. Ask: *Who is the illustrator?* (Dave McKean) Discuss other features such as the lack of chapter titles and the style of the font (edgy, sharp). Ask: *What is your first impression of the book?*

Chapters 1–5

Read page one of Chapter 1 aloud. Ask: *What have you found out?* (The Elder Paw, Varjak's grandfather, tells stories of their ancestor, Jalal, a warrior cat from Mesopotamia; Varjak is keen for adventures, though he's never left the Contessa's house.) Discuss whether their answers are factual (in context) or inferred. (The Elder Paw's relationship to Varjak is factual; Varjak's longing for adventures is inferred.) Invite children to read the rest of Chapter 1 while you build a chart of the characters. Refer to question 14 on the bookmark and encourage comments on looks matching personalities. Continue to add other characters to the chart, focusing on defining characteristics (for example, the Gentleman's full, wet pink lips, and their suggestions about his character). Ask: *Do looks define characters in real life?* (No!)

Invite groups to discuss question 2 on the bookmark and note clues in the next few chapters (for example, amber not green eyes, wants to go Outside and hunt, restless not content with dull life). Discuss question 3 on the bookmark. Ask: *What is a 'pedigree' cat?* (Pedigrees have traceable breed ancestors.) Survey whether the children have pets and whether any are pedigrees. Ask: *Does being a pedigree mean an animal is better?* (No, but definitely more expensive.) Draw children's attention to the book's illustrations – their silhouette, brush-stroke style. Periodically refer to question 15: the Gentleman and his cats, for example, underline the sinister atmosphere surrounding his arrival. Ask: *Why is the Gentleman drawn out of proportion?* (drawn from Varjak's perspective: low, looking up)

Ask children to read Chapters 2 to 5 in groups. Encourage them to 'read as writers' and list author writing techniques such as the rhetorical questions reflecting Varjak's thoughts, as on the first page of Chapter 2. Reading as a writer is an ongoing approach, so hold regular 'Class Councils' to exchange ideas. Begin a record of writing techniques, noting good examples with page numbers. Questions 10 to 13 on the bookmark encourage children to notice and appreciate some of these techniques.

Invite volunteers to summarise events so far and link to classic story structure (introduction and problem/challenge). On the last two pages of Chapter 5, promote enjoyment of how the layout and illustrations dramatise the moment, and share thoughts on Varjak's feelings as he sits on the wall.

Chapters 6–9

Chapter 6 opens with an engaging spread, underlining the integrated layout and illustrations. Focus on the detail created by a few strokes. Read Chapter 6 aloud, using expression to highlight how the author reflects Varjak's doubts and turmoil in the questions he asks himself, in the wind's voice taunting him and in his memory of his family's opinion of him. SF Said's rich language means almost any part of the book can be used as a mentor text. He uses vivid imagery, expressive verbs and patterns of three throughout, as well as more explicit visual cues, such as where Varjak falls from the tree: capitals, italics, exclamation marks, ellipsis, short one-line paragraphs and the dash from one page leading into a dash on the next page where the illustration mirrors blackness.

Chapter 7 is the first of seven dream chapters. At the start of Chapter 8, Varjak compares his old life to his present, visualising himself returning home as a hero. Ask: *What is Varjak's mood in Chapter 8?* Encourage evidence (for example, Varjak feels joyous – running, stretching and the splash of sunshine). In Chapter 9, Varjak is confronted by the reality of his limited experience. Ask: *What are the Vanishings?* (Encourage predictions, not guesses.) Ask: *How does Varjak put the First Skill into action?* (He admits that he knows nothing and asks for help.) Reflect on this as a life lesson for us too.

Dream chapters

The seven dream chapters (7, 10, 14, 17, 22, 25 and 31) enable Jalal, Varjak's wise, warrior ancestor, to mentor and support Varjak as he leaves his secure, familiar world and embarks on an uncertain, perilous quest. Ask the children to identify features that differentiate these chapters: several begin with single line paragraphs; grey, less defined illustrations reflect Varjak's subconscious state; dream chapters have no physical page numbers although they remain part of the timeline. Having read the dream chapters, ask: *Why are Varjak's dreams set in Mesopotamia?* (his and Jalal's origin) Ask: *What appears in all the dreams?* (conversations with Jalal, Mesopotamia, zigzag trees, the smell of cinnamon, the taste of date palms) Discuss question 16 on the bookmark and ask: *Is Mesopotamia real?* The meaning of 'real' is an underlying theme.

Chapters 11–20

Varjak learns from his dreams and demonstrates his learning when confronted by real-life challenges in Chapters 11 to 20, which follow his progress on his mission to find a dog and save his family. These chapters can be read in stages, as a class or in groups, but hold regular plenaries to share thoughts and ideas. Encourage children to investigate dialogue and use page markers to highlight examples for sharing. Ask: *How do speaking styles reflect the characters?* (verbs, vocabulary, syntax, formality and so on) To keep the plenaries focused, refer to question 5 on the bookmark and gather the evidence as the story unfolds. At the end of Chapter 20, ask: *What do you think has happened to Tam?* (probably something linked to the Vanishings)

Chapters 21–28

Chapter 21 builds tension towards the climax. What the Gentleman does to the animals is implied but never explicitly stated. Explore ideas about what is going on after reading the toy shop scene but avoid lingering on the darker aspects. Ask: *What seems real about the toy cat and what doesn't? Why is Holly so upset by Tam's disappearance?* (It reinforces her view that friends always let you down.) Read the end of Chapter 25 aloud, from where the 'monster' appears. Discuss question 7 on the bookmark. Ask: *What is a cliff-hanger ending?* (when the end of a chapter or episode leaves the main character in a difficult moment) *How does the author build tension leading to this cliff-hanger ending?* (vivid description of monster blocking the way out; intense, close-up illustration; verbs: ripped, bolted, scrambled, screamed; ellipses; italics; exclamation marks; question marks; short paragraphs; interspersed illustrations)

Cludge's portrayal implies that cats rely more on brains, and dogs more on brawn. Ask: *What implies this in the book?* (the way Cludge speaks and repeats himself; the sound of his name) *Do you agree with this portrayal?* In Chapter 21, Varjak's physical wounds began to heal. Ask: *By the end of Chapter 28, what other wounds have also begun to heal?* (the loss of a friend/family)

Chapters 29–35

The book's climax can be separated into two parts: the real, physical climax of confronting the Gentleman and his cats to save everyone, and the testing of Varjak's loyalty and friendship. Ask: *Was returning home all that Varjak imagined?* (Look for thoughtful answers.) Varjak slips back into familiar opinions (prejudices) and ways. Discuss Varjak's dilemma over Holly. Ask: *At the end of Chapter 30, what hints Varjak will do the right thing in the end?* (Jasmine's voice still sounds like milk but now sour milk.)

In the final dream chapter, ask: *What's changed in the illustrations? What message does this give?* (Change from grey to grey and black – joining Varjak's dream world with reality, implying he's learned from Jalal and can use the skills in his own life.) Discuss question 4 on the bookmark and reflect on why Varjak's family wouldn't join him. Challenge the class on whether they made a good choice.

Structure

Discuss question 6 on the bookmark. (Chapters 1–5, introduction and problem; Chapters 6–28, build up; Chapters 29–34, climax and resolution; Chapter 35, conclusion) The most striking element of the book's structure is how the dream chapters are integrated yet differentiated from the main plot action, and directly affect Varjak's transformation. Discuss question 9 (for example, the strong cast of characters and lines such as, 'So much lay ahead of them. Anything was possible now.').

Style

The book is ideal as a mentor text for third person narrative writing. Questions 10 to 13 on the bookmark can be used to guide discussions in almost every chapter. Discuss question 18 on the bookmark to emphasise the importance the visual aspects – not just illustrations, but also text features and layout. Experiment by reading a chapter aloud without the children following and then re-reading following the text. SF Said's writing, however, even without added effects, is replete with high-impact words and poetic

rhythm, making it ideal for reading as a writer as well as for meaning and enjoyment.

Setting

The book has three major settings: the Contessa's house, Outside and Mesopotamia (Varjak's dreams). Discuss question 17 on the bookmark and link it to the reality theme. Using Chapters 4, 5 and 27, discuss how Varjak's view of the wall round the Contessa's house changed. Ask: *Have you ever remembered something vividly, yet found it different on returning after some time?* (for example, a nursery playground at school or a park)

Characters

Ask children to discuss question 8 on the bookmark in groups and report back on their ideas. Talk about friendship, about who Varjak's friends are and what they teach him about friendship. Categorise major and minor characters, leaving room for personal opinion (for example, Cludge appears late in the book but becomes a friend and saviour; Sally Bones appears little but her reputation is almost as important as she is). The most difficult character to categorise is Jalal. Challenge the children. Ask: *Is Jalal a real character if he only appears in dreams?*

Themes

After reading, ask children to reflect on question 8 on the bookmark. Choose the most relevant themes for your class or separate children into groups and ask them to discuss and prioritise a list you provide (for example, friendship, being different, growing up, heroism, nobility, loyalty, reality, self-belief, the meaning of home). Some themes are more concrete than others but all are worth exploring. Demonstrate how to gather and present evidence relating to a theme using mind maps or other visual techniques.

SCHOLASTIC
READ & RESPOND
Bringing the best books to life in the classroom

Varjak Paw
by SF Said

Focus on...
Meaning

1. What genre is this book?

2. What clues in the first chapters suggest that Varjak is unlike the rest of his family?

3. What does being a Blue and 'doing what a Blue does' mean for Father? Is he right?

4. Why did Varjak choose his family over Holly when he returned to the Contessa's house?

5. What did Varjak learn on his quest and how did this change him?

Focus on...
Organisation

6. How would you group the chapters according to classic story structure?

7. Which chapters have 'cliff-hanger endings'?

8. What are the important themes running through the story?

9. How does the book's ending hint that it might be part of a series?

SCHOLASTIC
READ & RESPOND
Bringing the best books to life in the classroom

Varjak Paw
by SF Said

Focus on...
Language and features

10. How does the author use layout and text effects to add emphasis to the narrative?

11. Find and discuss examples where the author uses sentence type, length and structure effectively.

12. The author uses expressive verbs and adverbs to describe action and manner of speaking. Find and note examples.

13. Describe the different characters' conversational style.

Focus on...
Purpose, viewpoints and effects

14. How do the characters' appearances reflect their personalities?

15. Describe the style of the illustrations. What do they add to the story?

16. Why does Jalal appear only in Varjak's dreams? Is he real?

17. Are the Contessa's house and Outside more or less real than Mesopotamia?

18. Would you rather read the book or listen to it? Why?

Extract 1

- This extract exemplifies how the author integrates action and thoughts, enhanced by layout and punctuation. Read the extract with the children listening rather than following. Ask: *How is the wall both symbolic and real?* (known from unknown; a physical barrier) *What happens to the Elder Paw?* (The black cats attack and kill him.) *How does Varjak react?* (His instincts are to stay and help, but rational thoughts override his instincts.)

- Re-read the extract together, highlighting features on an enlarged copy. Ask: *Why does Outside start with a capital?* (It's used as a place name – proper noun.) In paragraph three, ask: *Who says 'No!'* (No one. It depicts Varjak's reaction.) Circle 'slashed' and 'swarmed'. Ask: *What other powerful, descriptive verbs are used?* (for example, 'coiled', 'churned', 'screamed', 'echoed', 'exploded', 'pumped', 'powered', 'Heaved') Discuss their impact and imagery. Ask children to identify examples of figurative language (for example, 'stomach churned', 'swarmed', 'like a broken toy').

- Focus on text effects. Ask: *How do layout and punctuation echo what happens?* (Look at single-line and single-word paragraphs, dashes, ellipsis, italics, rhetorical question.) Focus on sentence structure in the long paragraph with its final sentence flowing on, tangling Varjak's physical and mental feelings, building the tension, climaxing at the ellipsis.

- Read the pages from *Varjak Paw* in Chapter 5 from 'Latched onto…' to 'edge of the world', noting how the last two paragraphs appear on each page of a spread dominated by illustrations, setting the moment apart and drawing readers in (for effect). Brainstorm words to reflect the dramatic moment and how Varjak might be feeling (for example, triumphant, anticipation, momentous, full of possibility).

Extract 2

- Use an enlarged copy with the children following closely to read until 'Varjak shivered at the thought'. Ask: *How does Varjak feel in the first paragraph?* (paralysed by fear) Circle the dash and show how the pause mirrors Varjak freezing in his tracks. Underline 'froze' and ask: *Is it used figuratively or literally?* (figuratively) Re-read the first paragraph to demonstrate the rhythm created by repetition of 'they' and 'their'.

- Focus on personification. Ask: *What human-like characteristics are portrayed?* (for example: eyes – 'flicker', 'gaze'; 'Not asleep, but dead'; 'flank') Varjak sees monsters. *How do we know they are cars?* (infer using prior knowledge that Varjak lacks) Ask: *Why does Varjak 'shiver'?* (It demonstrates his fear and links to the cold imagery.) Ask: *What is the present tense of 'slunk'?* (slink) Ask: *What does 'gingerly' mean and what is the wordplay?* (with extreme care or delicacy; ginger is often associated with cats) Invite a volunteer to demonstrate Varjak's actions.

- Ask volunteers to read the remainder of the extract. Highlight 'monsters' and 'dogs' in the text. Ask: *Why does the author use the words almost interchangeably?* (Varjak sees them as monsters but believes they are dogs; it reflects his confusion.)

- Highlight words and imagery the children regard as especially effective. Point out the short, sometimes single-line paragraphs and the variety of sentence length and types. Examine the way they match what Varjak experiences and how he thinks, feels and reacts. Finally ask: *Why are some parts in italics?* (to indicate Varjak speaking to Jalal in his head rather than actually)

Extract 3

- Explain that groups of four will perform a dramatic reading of the extract. Set aside time to prepare, including who will read what. Encourage creativity – for example, around the italicised words.

- Let children annotate their copies to guide them. Explain that they should look out for 'directions' embedded in the text: dialogue and accompanying verbs such as 'urged', 'hissed', 'whispered'; the short, slightly choppy sentences, emphasising the tension; the dashes marking pauses/breaks within sentences; and the paragraphs switching from thoughts to action and back. Above all, highlight the way ellipses are used. Ask: *What are ellipses used for?* (to show omission; to create a pause for effect; to mark an unfinished thought; and, in plays, to indicate trailing off into silence) *How is it used here?* (pause for effect – in this case helping the action appear in slow motion) Explain that dashes can also be used for this.

- Ask: *Why is there a large gap before* 'Moving Circles!'*?* (to emphasise Slow-Time) *How long did it actually take between the monster springing and everything going black?* (seconds) Remind them that the three Skills mentioned were the ones the Elder Paw knew. Varjak has already learned the first two. Encourage them to predict the Skill to be learned in the next chapter.

- Finally, after practising, arrange for groups to do their readings to the class or to other groups, and then select groups to perform the reading for other classes to promote the book.

Extract 4

- Ask children to skim the extract. Ask: *What is the purpose of the extract?* (informative) *Is it fact or opinion based?* (fact) *Where would you expect to find this type of text?* (in an encyclopaedia or on an online reference site) Differentiate between fact and fiction. Ask: *How is this style of writing different from fiction?* (based on facts sourced from historical texts, artefacts and images; fiction is imaginative)

- Compare Mesopotamia here and in the book. Ask: *Was Mesopotamia a real place in history? What about in the story?* (Historically, it was real. In the story, it's reality-based to be authentic.) Display the media resources 'Images of ancient Mesopotamia' and 'Mesopotamia: then and now' to add context.

- Ask children to re-read the extract, underlining unfamiliar words like 'ziggurats' and referring to a dictionary and the images for support. Ask: *What are 'CE' and 'BCE' abbreviations for?* (Common Era; Before Common Era)

- Review structure and layout. Together, note the use of paragraphs to organise topics, bullets for listing and columns. Ask: *What is the benefit of including a map?* (geographically and historically locates an unfamiliar place)

- Lastly, focus on comprehension questions requiring analysis of the whole content. Ask: *Why was Mesopotamia successful?* (primarily, growth of cities and invention of writing, and other important advances and inventions) *Why is Mesopotamia known as the 'Cradle of Civilisation'?* (one of earliest documented empires, the development of cities) *Why did the author choose Mesopotamia for the Paws' origin?* (probably because it was known for domesticating cats)

Extract 1

Chapter 5

The Elder Paw was right. The only chance was to find a dog. His grandfather was doing what he had to; now it was all up to Varjak.

His mind on fire, Varjak tore his eyes from the garden, and turned to the wall. It separated the world he knew from the world Outside. No Paw had been over that wall since Jalal himself came from Mesopotamia, but it was the only way out.

He took a deep breath, coiled his body tight. One last glance, over his shoulder. No!

The black cats had caught the Elder Paw. They had him backed against the house. They came at him from both sides. He slashed out, but together they swarmed on top of him, and forced him to the ground.

There was a terrible howl. The black cats came away, shaking their heads. And the Elder Paw—

The Elder Paw looked limp, like a broken toy.

There was a roaring in Varjak's ears. His stomach churned. Everything inside him screamed at him to stay, to fight, to help the only cat who ever understood him. But the Elder Paw's words echoed in his mind: *go, before it's too late*. He turned to the wall.

Three.

Two.

One.

Varjak exploded into motion. Back legs uncoiled. Front paws reached out for a grip. Found it. Back legs pushed, pumped, powered up, up, and like the wind, Varjak Paw flew up the face of the wall, up, through the trees, higher than the curtains, higher than the house, up, beginning to tire, muscles aching, vision blurring – how much further? – up, grip after grip, paw over paw, slipping…

Latched onto a ledge. Heaved. And made it to the top of the wall.

Outside! For the first time since Jalal, a Paw stood on the edge of the world.

Extract 2

Chapter 12

Varjak stepped onto the pavement – and froze in his tracks. Before him, lined up on the edge of the road, was a whole column of shiny metal monsters. They stood in single file, stock still. They weren't moving, or making any sound. Their eyes were dull and lifeless, their round black wheels at rest.

But they were dogs – and this was Varjak's chance to talk to them.

'Excuse me,' he said.

They didn't react; not even a flicker in the eyes. Perhaps they were sleeping. He took a deep breath, and crept closer to them, ready to run if they suddenly awoke. He slunk onto the road, stretched out a paw, and gingerly touched a monster's smooth metal flank.

It was cold. Not asleep, but dead. Varjak shivered at the thought.

Far away, but closing in, something shrieked. Something roared. Varjak's heart thudded in his chest as he turned to face it. The shrieking, roaring noise grew louder. It was a pack of dogs, live ones, and they were coming down the road towards him.

He'd forgotten how fast and wild they were. In motion, they blurred beneath the street lights. Their yellow eyes were open, so round and bright they seemed to pierce his skull. He couldn't meet their gaze.

He had to look away. No wonder people were scared of them!

Varjak quaked as the monsters roared past, one after another after another. They were massive, mighty, unstoppable. In their wake came that foul, choking smell. It made him cough and cough and cough.

He cowered in the lethal wind; watched the red eyes at the back recede into the distance.

What should I do, Jalal?

Awareness, the Second Skill: *before you do anything, you must know what you are dealing with. Assume nothing; be sure of the facts.*

Extract 3

Chapter 24

Varjak's head was whirling. Sally Bones knew about Jalal. She knew about the Way, much more than he did. She wasn't even scared of this monster.

'Thanks for keeping quiet about the alleys,' said Holly. 'Come on, let's get out of here, before it gets us,' she urged.

The monster began to lumber towards them. Its big blunt claws clacked on the pavement as it came. It was incredibly powerful. Even its tail looked as if it could knock them senseless.

Varjak focused. What would Jalal do? Second Skill: Awareness. He looked into its eyes. They were cloudy black. There was pain in those eyes – and there was fear, almost terror, in its scent.

It barked again, a deafening sound. Varjak didn't flinch: he just kept looking into its eyes. If he hadn't once stood before a roaring dog, he would have run away. But compared to those metal monsters, this frightened, barking animal was friendly.

'What are you doing?' hissed Holly. 'Let's go!'

Varjak looked up. He could probably make it over a wall or onto a window ledge, like Sally Bones's gang. He gambled instead and trusted his instincts. This time, he wasn't going to run, he wasn't going to panic. He was going to stand his ground and face it down.

'Don't be afraid,' he said to the monster, in the calmest voice he could manage. It opened its jaws. They were big enough to swallow him whole. 'Don't be afraid,' he whispered.

And then it sprang at him…

Slow-Time!

… and Holly leaped for cover…

Moving Circles!

… but Varjak stood his ground…

Shadow-Walking?

… wrong.

The monster smashed into him. The world turned upside down – and everything in it went black again.

Extract 4

Mesopotamia

Mesopotamia, known as the 'Cradle of Civilisation, was located around two great rivers – the Tigris and the Euphrates. Geographically, today, it would encompass Iraq, Syria, Kuwait and areas along the Turkish-Syrian and Iran-Iraq borders. Over its history, spanning from BCE10,000 to around 637–640CE, Mesopotamia incorporated many cultures, empires and civilisations. Its success is often attributed

to the rise of the 'city' and its invention of writing (which also developed independently in Egypt and in China).

Unusually in those days, women had almost equal rights to men, owned businesses and traded freely.

Mesopotamia is believed to have been 'first' at many things, including:

- inventing the wheel (with leather tyres) and chariots
- developing advanced agriculture and irrigation

- domesticating animals, especially cats
- making wine and beer
- employing sophisticated weapons and warfare strategies
- harnessing wind to power boats.

In addition, Mesopotamians used 60, a number sacred to their god An, in many calculations familiar today, including marking time in hours, minutes and seconds, and geometry – 360 degrees in a full circle.

Mesopotamia was famed for its learning: reading, writing, religion, law, medicine and astrology were all taught in its many schools. It was also a religious society with numerous gods and the temple at the centre of everyday life. Priests – and later kings – ruled Mesopotamia as it developed from a hunter-gatherer society into a prosperous, multinational empire with over 1000 cities, characterised by sun-dried brick buildings and ziggurats.

Although it eventually became part of the Persian empire and, later still, the Greek and Roman empires, Mesopotamia's legacy has lasted into many areas of modern life.

GRAMMAR, PUNCTUATION & SPELLING

1. Relatively speaking

Objective

To use relative clauses.

What you need

Copies of *Varjak Paw,* interactive activity 'Relate', printable page 'Matching relatives', scissors, notebooks.

What to do

- While reading Chapter 1, ask: *Who are Varjak's relatives?* As children answer, draw a family tree on the board showing how Varjak is related to the other family members.

- Demonstrate how to join statements using a relative pronoun by writing on the board: 'Varjak is a cousin to Julius. Julius is also a cousin to Jasmine. Varjak is brother to Julius, who is cousin to Jasmine.' Point out that 'who' refers to Julius – it gives more information about him.

- Write these relative pronouns on the board: 'who', 'which', 'where', 'when', 'whose', 'that'. Explain that they introduce relative clauses that add information to clarify or add detail to nouns. They can also combine two or more sentences to help writing flow by joining sentences and avoiding repetition. 'Who' and 'whom' refer to people (as subject and object); 'which' refers to things, animals or ideas; 'that' and 'whose' are for people, animals, things and ideas.

- Open interactive activity 'Relate' and work through it as a class to practise using the pronouns.

- Hand out printable page 'Matching relatives' and ask children to cut out the starters, finishers and relative pronouns. Give them time to experiment and form sentences, before asking them to write them in their notebooks.

Differentiation

Support: Allow children to work in pairs on the sheet.
Extension: Encourage the children to invent alternative endings or starters to their sentences.

2. Dashes as brackets

Objective

To use dashes to indicate parenthesis.

What you need

Copies of *Varjak Paw.*

What to do

- Revise the difference between hyphens and dashes. Ask the children to identify hyphens on the first page of Chapter 9. Ask: *What do these hyphens do?* (join words to form compound adjectives) Ask: *In Chapter 1, what hyphenated synonym for pedigree also describes Varjak and his family?* ('pure-bred') Remind them that although dashes look similar to hyphens, dashes are longer and have a different function.

- Focus on two ways the author uses dashes to ensure a clear understanding: as brackets or to add an afterthought (additional but optional information). Write this example on the board: 'The words – Jalal's words – were safe in his head.' Then invite a volunteer to demonstrate how the dashes are used as brackets (in parenthesis). (Dashes work in pairs to enclose additional information, in this case clarifying whose 'words'.) Emphasise that words enclosed by dashes – like those inside brackets – must be able to be omitted without affecting the main sentence.

- Organise groups to find two examples of single dashes in Chapter 9 and discuss their use before sharing as a class. Ask groups to find examples in a chapter of their choice, noting page numbers and identifying how they are used.

- Hold a plenary session to review and discuss the examples.

Differentiation

Support: Specify a chapter for children to search (for example, Chapter 7 or 19).
Extension: Invite children to discuss the effect of the dashes in the final double spread of Chapter 12, then present to the class.

3. Introduce with a colon

Objective

To use a colon for introducing.

What you need

Copies of *Varjak Paw*, interactive activity 'Introductions', photocopiable page 22 'Colon introductions'.

What to do

- Draw a giant colon on the board with three arms. Invite examples of when to use a colon (introduce lists, dialogue in plays, or ideas/related information). SF Said regularly uses colons to introduce ideas/information and lists. Ask children to identify two examples of colon use in the first two pages of Chapter 19. Ask: *What is this colon doing?* (before 'why like this, not like that?' – introducing an idea, a question; after 'Everything began to glow' – introducing a list.)

- For the first example, ask: *Would the sentence still be complete if the questions the colon introduces were left out?* (yes – the questions are only examples) Highlight how the question after the colon does not start with a capital letter. Ask: *What items are listed in the second example?* ('ground', 'sky', 'water in the fountain') Note the absence of 'and' between the final two list items (the comma is followed directly by the noun phrase about 'water'). Ask: *What are all three items doing?* (beginning to glow)

- Ask groups to scan Chapters 3 to 5 for examples of colon use. Share findings, discussing the purpose of each use.

- Allow children to work through interactive activity 'Introductions' before they complete photocopiable page 22 'Colon introductions'.

Differentiation

Support: Allow pairs to discuss answers when completing the sheet.
Extension: Ask children to find and discuss where two colons are used in one sentence in Chapters 6 ('It was like walking on ice...') and 23 ('They all stared at him...').

4. Prefixes transform

Objective

To use the verb prefixes 'de', 'dis', 'mis', 'over' and 're'.

What you need

Copies of *Varjak Paw*, interactive activity 'Pick a prefix', printable page 'Prefixes at work'.

What to do

- Revise the difference between suffixes and prefixes. Write 'use' on the board and invite a volunteer to use it in a sentence as a verb. Draw arms out and show how the verb changes when you add a suffix (used, using, uses) or turn it into an adjective (useful). Write 'prefix' above and to the left of 'use' and ask: *What does 'pre' mean?* (before; for example, pre-school, preview, precook) *What prefixes can you add in front of 'use' to change its meaning?* (for example, 're', 'mis', 'dis', 'over', 'under') Draw an arm from each prefix to 'use' and trace the flow to show that both suffixes and prefixes can be added to the same root verb.

- Turn to Chapter 25. Ask: *What does Shadow-Walking allow a cat to do?* (disappear) What is the root verb in disappear? (appear) *What other prefixes could you use with appear?* (re) Point out that not all verbs can take a prefix.

- Open interactive activity 'Pick a prefix' and work through it as a class, or allow them to practise individually.

- Hand out printable page 'Prefixes at work' for the children to complete independently.

Differentiation

Support: Allow pairs to work on the sheet. If necessary, provide the word options for part two (agree, pay, took, bone, hearten, look turn).
Extension: Ask children to write sentences using verbs that can take more than one prefix – for example, appoint (dis, re) generate (de, re) – to demonstrate how each is used in context.

5. Rule of three

Objective

To use devices to build cohesion.

What you need

Copies of *Varjak Paw*, printable page 'Three rules!', photocopiable page 23 'Rule of three'.

What to do

- SF Said uses a range of techniques and grammatical patterns to add cohesion, within and across paragraphs. Read page two of Chapter 1, with the children following. Lightly emphasise 'no one' in each paragraph. Ask: *What does each paragraph describe?* (past, present scene, Varjak's opportunity – the future) *Which pronoun is repeated in all three paragraphs?* ('No one') Discuss the effect of the repetition. (links past, present and future)

- Many writing forms use 'rule of three' patterns: traditional tales frequently involve 'three' (for example, three little pigs, three wishes); plays often have three acts; slogans, sayings and jokes regularly focus on three. Write 'blood, sweat and tears' on the board. Ask: *What does it mean?* (hard work) Invite triplet examples from stories, sayings or advertising; for example, Three Blind Mice; faith, hope and charity; morning, noon and night; faster, higher, stronger (Olympic motto).

- Use printable page 'Three rules!' Encourage the children to underline and annotate key words as you discuss the author's use of repetition and the rule of three at word, sentence and paragraph level. (purpose/effect: emphasis, rhythm, more memorable)

- Hand out photocopiable page 23 'Rule of three'. Explain that the children must invent sentences or paragraphs that follow a similar grammatical pattern to each example given.

Differentiation

Support: Work with children to establish each rule of three on the photocopiable sheet before they start writing.
Extension: Encourage children to scan the book for other examples of the rule of three.

6. Which/witch one to use?

Objective

To distinguish between homophones and other words which are often confused.

What you need

Photocopiable page 24 'Use the right word', interactive activity 'It's confusing', sheets of paper or card.

What to do

- Revise: homophones – words sounding the same but spelled differently, for example, lesson (noun), lessen (verb); homonyms – words looking and sounding the same but serving different purposes, for example, bark (verb and noun) of a dog, bark (noun) of a tree; homographs – words looking the same, but sounding different and serving different purposes, for example, wind (noun), wind (verb).

- Invite children to write examples on sheets of paper or card to create a wall chart. Ask: *What do the pairs of words mean? What parts of speech are they? How do you know which is correct?* (context)

- Explain that context is important for pronunciation in speaking or reading aloud as well as for writing and spelling. Remind them that word pronunciation can be affected by accent, dialect and level of formality, and may not always help with spelling, especially with homophones or other easily confused words (near homophones).

- Open interactive activity 'It's confusing' and work through it together. As you work through, encourage children to suggest sentences to demonstrate how to use the other words from the drop-down choices. Add examples to the wall chart.

- Hand out photocopiable page 24 'Use the right word' for children to complete independently before discussing the answers as a class.

Differentiation

Support: Let children write a sentence for one of each pair of words on the sheet.
Extension: Encourage children to research other words to add to the wall chart.

Colon introductions

● Write a sensible ending to complete the sentence after each colon introduction.

1. The noisy monsters roared down the road:

   _____

2. Varjak remembered the most important skill of all:

   _____

3. Sally Bones frightened all the cats:

   _____

4. The Elder Paw told him to remember three things:

   _____

5. The future looked bright:

   _____

6. The café bins promised a good dinner:

   _____

7. Varjak at last knew what he was looking for:

   _____

8. Holly and Varjak explained what Tam had to do:

   _____

9. Varjak realised what was wrong with the toys:

   _____

Rule of three

● Underline the repetition, rule of three, or both in each example. Then write your own version, following a similar pattern.

1. 'The night was full of strange sounds too. Things were rumbling, bells ringing, sirens wailing.'

_____

_____

2. 'Still, he had to get on with his mission: find a dog, take it home, beat the Gentleman and his cats.'

_____

_____

3. 'He could be himself, he could be part of something, he could even have friends.'

_____

_____

4. 'He could smell food: salty, fishy, oily.'

_____

_____

5. Lightning flared up above. Thunder cracked. Rain streamed down Varjak's face like tears.

_____

_____

6. 'I'll show you how to hunt, to fight, to live Outside – if you come with me.'

_____

Use the right word

● Write a sentence using each word in the correct context. Use a dictionary to check your work.

1. queue _____

2. cue _____

3. seen _____

4. scene _____

5. prey _____

6. pray _____

7. where _____

8. wear _____

9. quite _____

10. quiet _____

11. their _____

12. there _____

13. they're _____

14. fears _____

15. fierce _____

PLOT, CHARACTER & SETTING

1. Build a descriptive collage

Objective

To describe a setting.

What you need

Copies of *Varjak Paw*, printable page 'Describe what you see', plain paper, poster board, thesauruses.

Cross-curricular link

Art

What to do

- Read the opening spread of Chapter 6. Ask: *Imagine you are Varjak. What do you see?* Encourage specific, factual answers focusing from foreground to background, noting how the detail in the illustration fades with distance.

- Read the description of the city in Chapter 6 in groups, then discuss how the illustrations bring the text alive, despite being silhouette-style sketches. Hand out printable page 'Describe what you see'. Re-read the text, asking writing technique questions as you go, encouraging children to underline words and features. Point out interesting words ('jumble', 'squat', 'jostled', 'loomed', 'bustling'), contrasts ('tall'–'squat'; 'gleaming'–'dark with chimney smoke'; 'wide open'–'narrow'; 'sharp pointy'–'soft, curved'), figurative language ('shining like silver'), and sentence length, variety and structure.

- Go outside. Position groups in different spots, and ask them to list and sketch what they see, near to far; they can add detail later. Back inside, ask groups to brainstorm and transform their factual list into descriptive writing, using the extract as a model. Demonstrate as necessary. Encourage them to use thesauruses to find interesting words.

- Invite children to build collages with pieces of paper containing their descriptive words, phrases and sentences, and their sketches. Encourage creativity.

Differentiation

Support and extension: Organise groups or allocate group roles strategically.

2. I am Holly

Objective

To consider how authors develop characters.

What you need

Copies of *Varjak Paw*, photocopiable page 29 'I am Holly', media resource 'Cats', printable page 'Character profile', notebooks.

Cross-curricular link

PSHE

What to do

- Invite a volunteer to describe someone (not from the class). Map characteristics as they are volunteered on the board, dividing them into physical and personality attributes. Ask prompt questions, if necessary, to develop a well-rounded description, such as: *What are they like to be with? How do feel when you are with them? What sort of voice/laugh/way of speaking do they have?* Discuss the characteristics and brainstorm ways to make them more descriptive, exploring similes, metaphors and words (adjectives, verbs, adverbs) to enhance the image. Add these to the character map.

- Ask pairs to read Chapter 9, where Varjak meets Holly. Provide photocopiable page 29 'I am Holly' and ask them to take notes about her (gravelly voice, spiky black-and-white fur, mustard-coloured eyes, younger than Jasmine or Julius but harder). Discuss findings, differentiating between personality-building information and physical descriptors (use media resource 'Cats').

- Ask children to use printable page 'Character profile' and their character map to write four short paragraphs on Holly in their notebooks. Encourage partners to edit each other's profiles.

Differentiation

Support: Allow pairs to write the profile.
Extension: Ask children to skim the book for additional information to extend Holly's profile.

3. Definitely dialogue

Objective

To investigate and perform dialogue.

What you need

Copies of *Varjak Paw*, interactive activity 'Speak', printable page 'Express yourself', sticky notes (optional), recording device (optional).

Cross-curricular link

Drama

What to do

- Re-read Chapter 1 to the class, using the textual cues to interpret the dialogue, while encouraging children to note down verbs and adverbs that indicate how the character speaks, particularly alternatives to 'said'. Share findings and ask: *What else suggests the tone and style of speaking?* (actions, for example, 'coming over and straightening his collar' or 'said Mother, smoothing and grooming')

- Briefly review dialogue punctuation using interactive activity, 'Speak': speech marks around words spoken, new line for new speaker, spoken words beginning with a capital, position of punctuation.

- Ask groups of three to perform a dramatic dialogue of Chapter 15. Explain they must read the chapter to identify the three speakers and analyse the dialogue (sticky notes can be helpful). Narrator parts are omitted. They can use printable page 'Express yourself' to guide their performance. Allocate practice time before they perform. If possible, record performances. Invite children to assess their performance and, if time, re-record it. Hold a final performance session, or screening of the recordings, to review how well they interpreted the dialogue.

Differentiation

Support: Spend time with groups, checking they have identified the dialogue correctly.
Extension: Invite children to investigate verbs, adverbs and actions that enrich dialogue and characterisation to perform the dialogue in Chapter 2 or another chapter of their choice.

4. Is it true about Sally Bones?

Objective

To predict what might happen from details stated and implied.

What you need

Copies of *Varjak Paw*, slips of paper.

What to do

- Read the two pages in Chapter 15 where Holly explains the street gangs and first mentions Sally Bones. Ask: *Why is Tam scared of Sally Bones?* (she's everywhere, not one of us, all white, can become invisible) Invite children to read Chapters 23 and 24 in groups and list things about Sally Bones – for example, her looks, abilities, effect. Ask children to identify anything factual in their lists that can be verified (for example, colour, one eye).

- Re-read the chapters as a class to identify techniques the author uses to portray Sally Bones as scary. (For example: her looks; names – Razor implies sharp and deadly, Bones implies death; contrasts – white fur and smell of darkness, dank and deadly things; her gang look like kittens; her actions and effect on others.) Encourage children to offer ideas as you go, using discretion over what to focus on. Ask: *How does Sally Bones react when Varjak mentions Jalal?* (interrogates him, fearful)

- Hand out slips of paper and ask the children to predict how Sally Bones might be linked to Jalal. Discuss ideas, making sure they link to the children's knowledge of the characters so far.

Differentiation

Support: Demonstrate how to use evidence to support predictions.
Extension: Encourage children to consider what Sally Bones means when she says 'You… Is it you?'

5. Mesopotamia for real

Objective

To summarise the main ideas drawn from more than one paragraph.

What you need

Media resources 'Mesopotamia: then and now' and 'Images of ancient Mesopotamia'.

Cross-curricular links

History, geography

What to do

- Display media resources 'Mesopotamia: then and now' and 'Images of ancient Mesopotamia'. Hand out Extract 4 and it read together. Ask: *Is this text mostly fact or opinion?* (fact)

- Give groups five to ten minutes to prepare, then ask a spokesperson from each group to summarise the extract's main points in one sentence per paragraph. Ask: *Was Mesopotamia real?* (yes) *How do we know?* (archaeology, artefacts, maps and writings)

- Ask groups to read the dream chapters (7, 10, 14, 17, 22, 25, 31) and list what they find out about Varjak's Mesopotamia. Ask: *What does Varjak experience* (include all the senses) *and find out about Mesopotamia?* (Tigris river with fish, hot nights, glimmering stars, zigzag trees, cinnamon smell, warm breeze, people cooking over a fire, crickets, reeds, walls, peaceful, feels like home) Collate findings. Ask: *Is this Mesopotamia real?* (Invite discussion and comparisons to Extract 4.) Encourage reflective and reasoned answers.

- Ask: *How does Varjak feel in his Mesopotamia?* (home, part of him) Ask children to choose sentences from Chapters 25 and 31 that demonstrate how Varjak feels and write them on slips of paper. Share ideas.

Differentiation

Support: Allow children to focus on either Chapter 25 or Chapter 31.
Extension: Encourage children to do their own research on Mesopotamia.

6. Varjak's hero journey

Objective

To identify and discuss conventions in writing.

What you need

Copies of *Varjak Paw*, photocopiable page 30 'Journey to be a hero'.

Cross-curricular link

History

What to do

- Ask: *What makes a hero? Can you think of examples in fiction, and in real life?* (Suggest heroes, especially current ones, both female and male.) Ask: *Is Varjak Paw a hero? Why?* (Yes. Encourage answers supported by evidence.)

- Draw an inverted 'V' on the board. Link events in the plot to classic story structure stages (introduction, problem, build up, climax, resolution, conclusion), by asking: *Where does the plot begin? What characters are introduced? What's the problem? What must Varjak do? Where does he go? What happens to him? What difficulties and dilemmas does he face? How does he resolve the problem?*

- Heroes in both traditional and modern stories often go on journeys – physical or ones of self-discovery, usually both – where they face challenges, learn about themselves, and become better people or grow up. Ask: *What stories can you think of?* (For example, the myth of Hercules, *The Hobbit*, *Star Wars*, *Harry Potter*, *The Hunger Games*, *Percy Jackson*.) Hand out photocopiable page 30 'Journey to be a hero'. Check understanding of the phases, then ask pairs to skim through the book and match chapters to phases in Varjak's hero journey, giving each chapter a title to identify it. Share ideas, especially how they handled the dream chapters.

Differentiation

Support: Work through the plot structure with selected groups before they tackle the sheet.
Extension: Encourage children to add detail to their plot of Varjak's journey.

7. Coming of age

Objective

To explain and discuss their understanding of what they have read.

What you need

Copies of *Varjak Paw*, photocopiable page 31 'Coming of age'.

Cross-curricular link

PSHE

What to do

- *Varjak Paw* is a coming-of-age story. Although a cat, Varjak has human characteristics, needs, feelings and even fears, making him easy to empathise with. Ask: *Is Varjak happy at the start of the story?* (not really; restless and longs for things his family doesn't) Ask: *Is he well cared for?* (practically, yes – he's fed and cared for but his family doesn't understand or nurture him, except for Elder Paw)

- Give small groups about ten minutes to skim the first four chapters to review what Varjak is like: what he thinks, feels, wishes and how he reacts. Ask a spokesperson from each group to summarise findings. Ask: *What adjectives describe him?* (for example, young, restless, lonely, dissatisfied)

- Hand out photocopiable page 31 'Coming of age'. Explain that groups are going to explore how Varjak changes through the book. (Note this activity could be done at the end of the book or as an ongoing activity as you read the novel.) Children use the Seven Skills to chart how Varjak changes as he learns new skills and applies them in his own life. Groups should then prepare a presentation, involving each group member, on how Varjak changes and what he learns about himself, using their completed sheet as notes.

Differentiation

Support: Consider groupings carefully and spend extra time with certain groups.
Extension: Encourage children to prepare a visual element using presentation software.

8. Endings

Objective

To identify and discuss conventions in writing by investigating beginnings and endings.

What you need

Copies of *Varjak Paw*, printable page 'Endings', notebooks.

What to do

- Do a favourite book survey and ask: *How did it begin? How did it end?* Demonstrate with a familiar book, perhaps a previous class reader. Summarise where and when (how much later), and so on, and then allow groups to tell each other about their favourite book. Share ideas and identify recurrent features, such as beginning and ending in the same place, whether loose ends are neatly tied up. Ask: *What books have you read that are part of a series? Does it matter if you read the second or third book without having read the first? Why?* (Encourage reasoned answers supported by examples.)

- Ask groups to read Chapter 35 together and then discuss the questions on printable page 'Endings' before answering in their notebooks.

- Ask: *How does this ending indicate the book has a sequel?* (Varjak doesn't stay with his family; Holly, Tam and Cludge go with him; many of the freed cats follow 'like they were leaders of a gang'; it suggests so much lies ahead of them.) Based on the ending, encourage the children to predict events, the setting and characters that will appear in the sequel *The Outlaw Varjak Paw*.

Differentiation

Support: Allow children to answer only the factual questions on the sheet.
Extension: Encourage children to analyse another book's ending, using similar questions.

I am Holly

- Note down information about Holly from Chapter 9 to fill in the character map. Then draw a picture of Holly.

🐾 **How she looks:**

🐾 **How she speaks/sounds:**

🐾 **Attitude:**

🐾 **Mannerisms:**

Holly

🐾 **Effect on Varjak:**

🐾 **Other information:**

🐾 **Words and phrases:**

Journey to be a hero

- Group the chapters into paw prints of Varjak's hero journey. Then summarise the events in each paw print.

Chapters   **Summary of events**

The ordinary world

Call to adventure

Fear of unknown – uncertainty

Meeting a mentor

Crossing the threshold – into the
unknown

Allies, enemies & tests

Supreme ordeal

Return home

Making amends

Coming of age

● Fill in the chart to use as notes for your presentation.

Adjectives to describe Varjak at the start of the book:

The Way	How Varjak applies the skill:
First Skill: *Open mind*	
Second Skill	
Third Skill:	
Fourth Skill:	
Fifth Skill:	
Sixth Skill:	
Seventh Skill:	
Mentor and friends:	
Lessons learned:	
Adjectives to describe Varjak at the end of the book:	

TALK ABOUT IT

1. Tell a story

Objective

To gain, maintain and monitor the interest of the listener(s).

What you need

Copies *Varjak Paw*, photocopiable page 35 'Story map', printable page 'Telling stories'.

What to do

- Read the first page of Chapter 1. Focus on the first sentence. Ask: *Is this a good way to begin a novel? Why?* (Guide their responses; yes, the idea of a story is appealing to most.) *How does Varjak feel about the Jalal stories?* (he loves them, they make him feel restless, he wants to be like Jalal)

- In Chapter 4, the Elder Paw explains that these tales have been 'passed down through the ages from Paw to Paw'. Discuss how stories are passed on in families and cultures. In the past, stories were told from memory rather than written down, which meant there was no exactly 'right' version. Ask: *Can you think of any well-known stories that have been around for generations?* (for example, fairy stories, myths, legends)

- Ask the children to think of a familiar story. On the board, demonstrate how to write a key-word story map and use it to tell a short story.

- Invite the children to complete story maps using photocopiable page 35 'Story map', then to recount their stories in small groups, using tips from the printable page 'Telling stories', before asking three questions to check if their audience was listening.

Differentiation

Support: Ask children to focus on retelling a well-known myth, legend or fairy story.
Extension: Invite children to tell their stories to a different or larger audience.

2. Of monsters and motorcars

Objective

To use relevant strategies to build their vocabulary.

What you need

Copies of *Varjak Paw*, thesauruses, photocopiable page 36 'Similarities and differences', interactive activities 'Synonyms' and 'Comparisons'.

What to do

- Write 'Monster' and 'Car' on the board. Refer to Chapter 4 from 'Then listen carefully…'. Ask: *How did the Elder Paw describe the monster called a dog?* Write the answers on the board under the heading 'Monster'. ('huge', 'strong enough to kill a man', they 'fill the heart with fear', 'foul breath', 'deafening sound')

- In Chapter 8, Varjak mistook a car for a dog. Ask: *Why did Varjak think the car was a dog?* (matched Elder Paw's description; see above) Write up the key words under 'Car' ('huge', 'big enough to kill a man', 'breath was foul', 'deafening', 'filled his heart with fear'). Ask: *What should have made Varjak realise the car wasn't a dog?* (Encourage reasoned answers.) Use Chapter 12 to find further words describing cars to add to the board (for example, 'shiny', 'metal flank', 'fast', 'unstoppable'). Identify differences and similarities.

- Revise how to use a thesaurus to find interesting synonyms. If time, work through the interactive activity 'Synonyms'.

- Hand out photocopiable page 36 'Similarities and differences' and explain how a Venn diagram works to depict similarities and differences. Encourage rich vocabulary, including compound words (such as 'man-eating') and short phrases. Share ideas.

Differentiation

Support: Let the children complete the interactive activity 'Comparisons'.
Extension: Discuss personification and let children write a personification poem.

3. Making rules

Objective

To participate actively in collaborative conversations.

What you need

Copies of *Varjak Paw*, poster paper.

Cross-curricular link

Citizenship

What to do

- Begin by discussing rules. Ask: *At school/home, who makes the rules?* (head of family, head teacher) *When else do we have rules?* (games, sports) *Why are rules important?* (keep order/peace, give parameters/ limits, to be fair) Invite volunteers to give examples of important rules outside of school. (for example, wear a helmet when riding a bike) *Are rules always sensible?* (Encourage discussion.)

- Varjak felt trapped by his family's and the house's 'unwritten' rules. Talk about 'unwritten rules' and where they come from. Ask: *How do we know what they are?* Ask pairs to find examples of unwritten rules in the first few chapters. (don't go Outside, wear a collar, don't climb the curtains, respect your elders) Share findings.

- Read Chapter 15. Ask: *According to Holly, what rules apply in the city centre?* (the centre is neutral; Ginger is boss of east side, Sally Bones of the west) *Why are these rules important?* (life or death)

- Hand out poster paper to groups. Invite them to consider ten important rules for keeping pets, covering all aspects of pet care.

- Encourage groups to compare rules with another group before a spokesperson from each group explains their rules and why they are important. Encourage questions from the class.

Differentiation

Support: Work with one or two groups to help them compare rules.
Extension: Challenge children to prioritise their rules from most to least important.

4. Cats vs dogs: it's debatable

Objective

To participate in discussions and debates.

What you need

Copies of *Varjak Paw*, photocopiable page 37 'Cats vs dogs', printable page 'Hold a debate'.

Cross-curricular link

Citizenship

What to do

- Write the headings 'Cats' and 'Dogs' on the board. Have a quick vote to see who prefers cats and who prefers dogs. Write the totals on the board. Have another vote. Ask: *Which are cleverer: cats or dogs?* Write the results on the board. Ask: *Who is correct?* (no correct answer; everyone is entitled to their opinion)

- Read Chapters 26 and 27. The author seems to convey cats in one way and dogs in another. Ask: *What opinion does the author seem to have about cats and dogs? How can you tell?* (Cats are portrayed as noble, sophisticated, intelligent; dogs as big, scary, clumsy.) Do you agree with SF Said's view? (Encourage opinions backed by examples, and debate.)

- Hand out photocopiable page 37 'Cats vs dogs' to small groups. Each group should choose one side of the argument and brainstorm four or five points in support of it. Each point must be supported with factual evidence or an example from experience.

- Organise opposing groups to hold a debate, following the guidelines on printable page 'Hold a debate'. Each team member should have a chance to speak. Invite volunteer teams to hold their debate in front of the class.

Differentiation

Support: Allow each child to present a separate speech.
Extension: Allow the class to judge which team wins the argument.

5. Finding out

Objective

To develop understanding through imagining and participating in role play.

What you need

Copies of *Varjak Paw*, printable page 'Interview sheet'.

Cross-curricular link

Citizenship

What to do

- Read Chapter 1 aloud, until just before the Gentleman arrives. Then invite two volunteers to role play an interview with you. They must answer your questions as if they were Varjak or Father, using the context in Chapter 1 and their imagination. Questions for Varjak: *Where were you going? Why did you disobey your parents? Why can't you stay inside like the others? Do you think Father always knows best?* Questions for Father: *Why isn't Varjak allowed Outside? Have you ever been Outside? When? Why must the family stay inside? Why do you think Varjak's ideas and how he behaves are wrong?*

- Remind the children about question types, especially open and closed questions: an interview should focus on open questions as they provide listeners with details.

- Read Chapter 35. At the end, some cats choose to stay and some choose to go. Encourage the children to imagine being an interviewer on the scene. Their job is to find out who is staying or leaving and why. Using printable page, 'Interview sheet', pairs role-play interviews, taking turns to be the interviewer. They should ask each other different questions from the sheet and be 'in character' when they answer.

Differentiation

Support: Choose characters for the children to interview and demonstrate 'in character' answers.

Extension: Invite children to prepare other 'open' questions to ask each other.

6. Identifying themes

Objective

To participate in presentations.

What you need

Copies of *Varjak Paw*, printable page 'Theme card'.

Cross-curricular link

PSHE

What to do

- Remind children that every story has at least one theme running throughout it. Explain that to identify a theme, they should ask, 'What did the character/s learn?' or 'What did I learn?' Display these two questions on the board. Themes can be summarised by key words like 'friendship', expressions like 'Truth will out', statements like 'It's ok to be different' or questions like 'What is real?'

- In discussion groups, ask children to take turns answering both questions on the board. For the first question, suggest a focus on characters like Varjak, Holly and Father. Guide them on how to use their answers to discuss and identify possible themes in the story.

- Share ideas. Display the suggested themes on the board; include the examples above and any others (for example, friendship, being different, growing up, heroism, authority, nobility, reality, self-belief, pride, home, a friend in need is a friend indeed).

- Hand out printable page 'Theme card'. Invite children to use the theme card to prepare and deliver a presentation about a theme in the book, giving evidence from the story and adding their own thoughts, reflections and opinions. Once they have prepared and practised, ask them to present to the class. Display the theme cards around the class.

Differentiation

Support: Work through a selected theme with small groups, helping them find appropriate evidence.

Extension: Encourage children to complete and present more than one theme card.

Story map

● Use key words to make notes about the story you will tell.

Setting:	Characters:

Opening sentence:

Beginning:	Middle:	End:

● Three questions about the story:

1. _____

   _____

2. _____

   _____

3. _____

   _____

Similarities and differences

- Find words in Chapters 4, 8 and 12 that describe cars, dogs and monsters. Write each word into the correct area of the Venn diagram. Follow the examples.
- Use a thesaurus to add synonyms to grow your vocabulary.

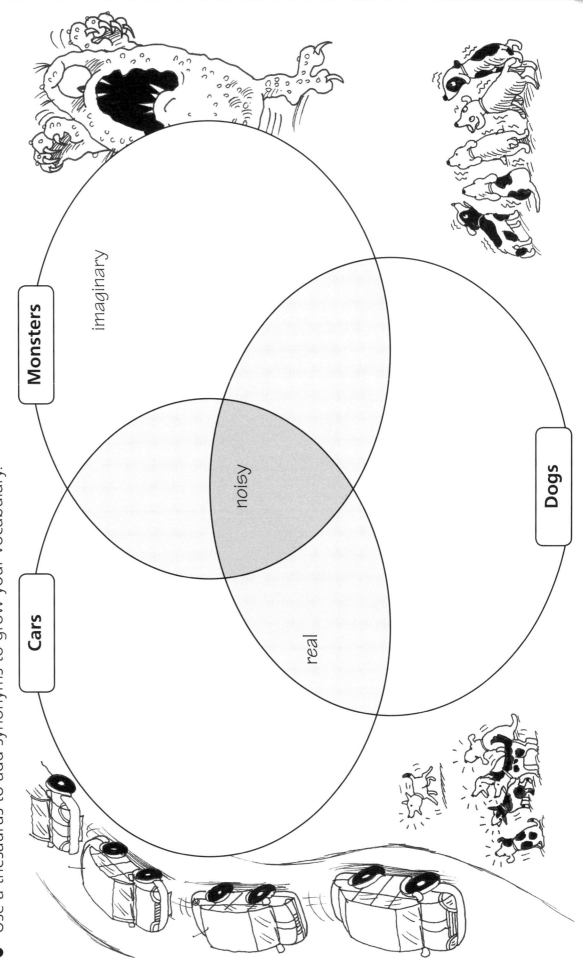

Monsters

imaginary

Cars

noisy

real

Dogs

Cats vs dogs

- Fill in the missing words to make a statement you support.

> We believe _____ are more intelligent
>
> than _____ for the following reasons…

- Write at least four points to support this statement and provide examples and evidence.

1. Point: _____

   Examples and evidence: _____

   _____

   _____

2. Point: _____

   Examples and evidence: _____

   _____

   _____

3. Point: _____

   Examples and evidence: _____

   _____

   _____

4. Point: _____

   Examples and evidence: _____

   _____

   _____

5. Point: _____

   Examples and evidence: _____

   _____

   _____

GET WRITING

1. Comma crazy

Objective

To use commas to clarify meaning or avoid ambiguity in writing.

What you need

Printable page 'Describe what you see', photocopiable page 41 'Break it up', coloured markers.

What to do

- Hand out printable page 'Describe what you see' and re-read the extract together. Ask: *What is the context of this extract?* (Varjak has just escaped and sees what is over the wall for the first time.)

- Ask the children to highlight the commas in the text. Ask: *How do the commas affect how you read the text?* (create pauses to give expression and clarify meaning) *Is the comma used for the same purpose each time?* (no) Together, find examples of different comma uses and revise the rules. Write them on the board: to separate words or phrases in a list; in place of brackets; after introductory words or phrases like 'Firstly'; before and after linking words like 'however' to create complex sentences.

- Ask pairs to complete photocopiable page 41 'Break it up'. Share and discuss answers.

Differentiation

Support: Encourage children to add one or two more sentences using commas.
Extension: Invite the children to write their own descriptions about a city, using commas for effect. Display them in the classroom.

2. Frame it

Objective

To discuss writing to learn from its structure and to use devices to build cohesion.

What you need

Copies of *Varjak Paw*, media resources 'Cars' and 'Comic strip features', notebooks.

Cross-curricular link

Art and design

What to do

- Invite the children to scan Chapter 12, focusing on illustration. Ask: *What story do the illustrations tell?* (car approaching, getting closer, looking increasingly dangerous, speeding past) *Are they important to understand the story?* (They enhance it and bring cohesion.) Ask: *Can you imagine this as a scene in a film?* (Discuss the visual impact.) Open media resource 'Cars' and discuss the characteristics or visual impact of each and the likely context (not all in fiction).

- Read aloud from '*What should I do, Jalal?*' to the end of Chapter 12. Ask: *Describe the paragraphs.* (short, pacey) Find examples of one- or two-line paragraphs. Ask: *What effect do they have?* (add emphasis) Identify the exclamation marks, noticing the increase as cars get closer, helping build tension.

- Ask the children to identify the chapter climax and discuss how the author accomplishes it. (double-page picture spread, spacing, single-word lines, punctuation)

- Display media resource 'Comic strip features'. Guide children to plan a short, dramatic scene as a comic strip in their notebooks. It can be an existing or invented scene. The pictures, dialogue and text in the strip should cohere, leading to a climax.

Differentiation

Support: Ask children to rewrite the car scene as a comic strip.
Extension: Ask children to rewrite and edit their comic strips in short paragraphs.

3. Sensing tension

Objective

To select appropriate grammar and vocabulary to enhance meaning.

What you need

Copies of Varjak Paw, interactive activity 'Tone it'.

What to do

- Draw an empty mind map on the board with the word 'tension' in the middle and six arms extending out. Discuss as a class what is meant by 'sixth sense'. (intuition or awareness). On each of the arms write the five senses and add the term 'sixth sense'.

- Read Chapter 16 aloud with expression. Focus on the part where Varjak turns away: 'Stung by Holly's words, he followed his senses down a turning off the street.' From this point in the chapter, brainstorm what he hears, sees, smells, feels, tastes and senses. Add ideas to the mind map. Then read Chapter 13 aloud and add further responses to the mind map.

- Ask children to identify writing techniques used to build tension (for example: setting – dark, lonely alleyway; tone – changes from light-hearted to serious/dangerous; punctuation – ellipses, colons, exclamation marks; sentence length – mainly short statements and questions; vocabulary – serious, dark; images – opposites, comparisons). Work through interactive activity 'Tone it' to practise and reinforce some of these techniques.

- Invite children to plan and write their own 'alleyway' event, starting: 'Varjak followed his senses down a turning off the street…' They should use at least one of the writing techniques discussed and answer the questions: *What did he see/hear/smell/feel/taste/ sense?*

Differentiation

Support: Invite children to plan and practise the story orally in groups before writing it down.
Extension: Ask children to read their stories aloud with expression. Encourage the class to say if they felt the tension.

4. Cat files

Objective

To use organisational and presentational devices to structure text.

What you need

Media resource 'Russian Blue', printable page 'Cat facts', Extract 4, photocopiable page 42 'Cat factfile'.

Cross-curricular link

Geography

What to do

- Begin by asking: *Who has a cat? Where did you get it? Would you like one?* Discuss differences between pet cats, street cats and pedigree cats. (A pedigree animal has a certified line of descent.)

- Display the cat picture in media resource 'Russian Blue'. Varjak is a Mesopotamian Blue. No such breed exists, but the Russian Blue is similar-looking.

- Organise the children into pairs and hand out copies of printable page 'Cat facts' for them to cut up and organise into sensible categories like physical features, history, pet care. Review their ideas.

- Refer to Extract 4 and hand out photocopiable page 42 'Cat factfile'. Ask: *What do you notice about how they are set out?* (organised; place for headings, paragraphs and picture) *What style of writing should be used?* (formal, factual, easy-to-read, full sentences) *Describe the presentation.* (neat, formal, uncluttered text and visual mix)

- Ask the children to use the printable and photocopiable pages (and other resources) to create a factfile using their own words. Use the factfiles for a wall display.

Differentiation

Support: Ensure children group the facts sensibly in their factfiles.
Extension: Ask groups to research a pedigree cat. Each child takes responsibility for a different aspect, then groups pool the information to produce and present a factfile.

5. Vanishings conundrum

Objective

To recognise structures that are appropriate for formal speech.

What you need

Copies of *Varjak Paw*, media resources 'Cat detective agency' and 'Missing', photocopiable page 43 'Investigation report'.

Cross-curricular link

Citizenship

What to do

- Open media resource 'Cat detective agency' (an advertisement). Ask: *What do the words 'feline' and 'felon' mean?* (feline – of the cat family; felon – someone who has committed a serious crime) *What service does it offer?* (detective services)

- Give children the following scenario: 'Something is threatening the safety of street cats – the Vanishings. Friends are disappearing and they don't know why. Imagine you are from the Fe-Fi-Fo agency, and concerned cats have asked you to investigate the Vanishings and compile a report.'

- Groups conduct the investigation, going through the book to find any mention of the Vanishings and making notes. They then use it to write reports using photocopiable page 43 'Investigation report' to help plan. Remind them of features of formal writing and report structure: title, introduction, paragraphs, conclusion; bullet points, headings, visuals such as maps, photographs and diagrams; factual, formal language (no contractions, colloquial terms, expressions or emotive language), past tense (except direct quotes) and mostly reported speech.

Differentiation

Support: Provide key sentences on the board to copy as starter sentences.

Extension: Invite children to design a 'missing' poster using the facts from the report and media resource 'Missing' as a model. Encourage a focus on detailed description and defining characteristics.

6. The Eighth Skill

Objective

To describe settings, characters and atmosphere, integrating dialogue.

What you need

Copies of *Varjak Paw*, notebooks, printable page 'Chapter plan'.

Cross-curricular link

Art and design

What to do

- Arrange the class into seven groups. Ask each group to read one of the seven dream chapters and summarise the dream in their notebooks: characters, setting, atmosphere (mood), dialogue (what is talked about), lesson (what Varjak learns).

- Invite a spokesperson from each group to present, in chronological order, the dream summaries. Review the similarities among the dreams (for example: wording, 'Varjak dreamed'; characters and setting; mood; Varjak learns a new skill).

- Explain they must imagine that the Way has an Eighth Skill, and that Varjak has one more dream to learn about it from Jalal. Invite children to write the new dream chapter. Hand out printable page 'Chapter plan' and demonstrate how to use it to plan the new chapter.

- Having planned, ask children to write a draft, focusing on creative vocabulary and imagery to recreate the mood and dialogue, and using the dream chapters as a model. Encourage them to edit their own and others' work before holding a reading of their chapters for a group or the class. If time, they can write out and illustrate their chapters in the style of *Varjak Paw*.

Differentiation

Support: Allow children to choose one of the existing dreams to rewrite in their words.

Extension: Encourage children to focus particularly on the dialogue: to punctuate it correctly and make it in character.

Break it up

- Read each sentence and decide if it needs one or more commas. Add them in with a coloured pen.

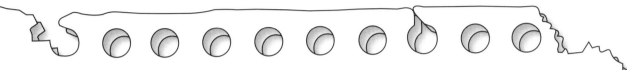

1. Varjak climbed up up up the face of the wall.

2. He climbed higher than the trees higher than the house higher than the Gentleman's cats until he reached the top.

3. From the top of the wall he could see for miles and miles.

4. In the distance beyond the park Varjak saw a city.

5. The city looked like a big busy bustling confusion of shapes and sounds.

6. He noticed tall towers long tunnels winding roads square houses and large flat billboards.

7. He sat quietly staring out over the city wondering if this place ever slept.

8. His whiskers twitched with anticipation fear excitement.

9. Finally he headed down the hill.

10. About this time back at the house his family would be waking up.

11. Next they would wash themselves and eat breakfast.

12. Finally Varjak felt free from all that fuss and bother.

13. It felt he thought like this was where he was meant to be.

14. Running rolling scrambling down the hill he went.

Cat factfile

● Sort the facts on the sheet 'Cat facts', then rewrite them as paragraphs into the correct places below. Try to use your own words.

Cat FACTFILE

Name:

Description:

Historical background:

Pet care:

Temperament and general characteristics:

Picture:

Investigation report

● Use the information you have gathered from *Varjak Paw* to complete this report on the missing cats.

FE-FI-FO Detective Agency
Feline Felon Finders

Report title:
Introduction: The agency was asked to investigate…
Findings: While conducting our investigation, the following information was gathered. (Photos, pictures and maps available on request.) 1. 2. 3. 4. 5.
Further evidence suggests…
Summary based on the findings:

ASSESSMENT

1. Explain the text

Objective

To understand what they read.

What you need

Copies of *Varjak Paw*, photocopiable page 47 'Read and understand', printable page 'Read and understand (answers)'.

What to do

- Explain that the children are going to complete a reading task to check their understanding of a text through different types of questions. Revise the different types and levels of questions: closed questions require simple 'yes' or 'no', right/wrong responses; open questions require detail, thinking and even opinion; multiple-choice questions require selection of an answer from ones provided. Explain that basic-level questions require an answer found directly from the text; middle-level questions require children to analyse information or classify; higher-level questions ask children to interpret and apply the information from the text. All these can include visual literacy elements.

- Remind them that, with a comprehension task, they should always: first, skim and scan the text for clues on what it is about (the context); second, read the text in detail; third, read through the questions; finally, read the text again. Once they have followed these steps, they will be ready to begin writing answers. You can write these steps on the board for them to follow.

- Hand out copies of photocopiable page 47 'Read and understand' with questions on Chapter 11. Read the chapter and questions together and then give a reasonable time limit to complete the exercise. Answers can be found on printable page 'Read and understand (answers)'.

Differentiation

Support: Read the questions with the children and check they understand them. Provide additional time to complete, if appropriate.

2. Let's talk

Objective

To select and use appropriate registers for effective communication.

What you need

Copies of *Varjak Paw*, printable page 'Dialogue matters'.

Cross-curricular link

Citizenship

What to do

- Ahead of the lesson, choose six children to prepare a reading of the following three dialogues: Chapter 7, from 'Welcome to the land of your ancestors…' to '… I will teach you'; Chapter 9, from 'What's your name?' to 'Just don't talk to me about dogs'; Chapter 26 from 'There was no escape now' to 'FRIENDS! FRIENDS!'

- Introduce the lesson by asking these children to read their prepared dialogues to the class. Discuss the dialogues. Ask: *What is the context of each dialogue?* (Chapter 7, a dream; Chapter 9, a hut/shelter from the storm; Chapter 26, an alleyway.) *What common activity are the characters doing?* (introducing themselves) *How would you describe each dialogue – formal or informal?* (The dialogue with Jalal in Chapter 7 is formal but the other two are informal.) *How can you tell?* (Discuss the difference in vocabulary, tone and subject matter. Also, note who is involved: Jalal is an elder, whereas Holly and Cludge are Varjak's peers.)

- Organise children into pairs or groups of three. Invite them to choose a dialogue from the story to prepare and present to the class. Their expression and tone should match the dialogue. Refer to the printable page 'Dialogue matters' for assessment criteria.

Differentiation

Support: Allow children to prepare and read aloud one of the dialogues previously presented.
Extension: Invite children to write and present their own dialogue from anywhere in the story.

3. Working suffixes

Objective

To convert nouns or adjectives into verbs using suffixes.

What you need

Interactive activity 'Making verbs', notebooks.

What to do

- Begin with a quick revision quiz. Call out five nouns, five adjectives and five verbs, mixed up. The children write down which they are. When checking the answers together, invite volunteers to give a definition of a noun, an adjective and a verb. If time, revise different types of nouns, verb tenses and subject–verb agreement.

- Revise root words and suffixes. Ask: *What suffixes can be added to these nouns to form adjectives: 'beauty', 'right', 'hate', 'sorrow', 'sense', 'love', 'topic'?* (ful, ible, able/ing, al)

- Explain that some suffixes can change nouns and adjectives into verbs: ise, ate, ify, en. Ask: *Using these suffixes, what verbs can you make from these nouns and adjectives: 'character', 'class', 'hyphen', 'dark'?* ('characterise', 'classify', 'hyphenate', 'darken') Ask volunteers to turn these words into verbs using suffixes: 'active', 'false', 'summary'. ('activate', 'falsify', 'summarise') Ask: *Why did the spelling of the root word change?* (spelling rule: the final letter (e or y) falls away because the suffixes begin with a vowel)

- Open the interactive activity 'Making verbs' and ask children to complete the three activities to revise and reinforce.

- Assess the children. Display a number of nouns and adjectives on the board for them to convert into verbs using suffixes. Spelling must count.

Differentiation

Support: Allow children to use dictionaries to check their spellings.
Extension: Challenge the children to use the verbs in a sentence.

4. Dear Diary

Objective

To identify the audience for and purpose of the writing, selecting the appropriate form.

What you need

Copies of *Varjak Paw*, media resources 'Dear Diary' and 'My first night Outside', notebooks.

Cross-curricular link

History

What to do

- Refer to the story. Ask: *Who tells the story?* (a narrator) *First or third person?* (third) *What tense is used?* (past) *Describe the structure.* (novel, chapters, plot, setting, characters)

- Open media resource 'Dear Diary' and read it aloud. Ask: *Who is the writer?* (Varjak) *How is it different from the novel?* (first person, past and present tense, diary, conversational tone) *Name other diary-style books.* (for example, *Diary of a Wimpy Kid, Anne Frank: The Diary of a Young Girl, The Diary of a Killer Cat, Zlata's Diary*) *What is the appeal of this form of writing?* Encourage discussion.

- Highlight important features of diaries: written in character (first person); entries are consistent with the writer/subject; past, present and future tense used to record events, express emotions and wishes/ambitions; talks about 'then' and 'now'; informal, chatty, conversational tone.

- Invite children to choose an event or chapter in the book and to write a diary entry in the character of Varjak. Assess their ability to capture Varjak when writing in character (first person).

Differentiation

Support: Provide sentence starters: 'Today I saw…', 'I spoke to…', 'I felt … when…'
Extension: Invite children to adapt their diary entry into a chapter of autobiography. Use media resource 'My first night Outside' as a model, demonstrating the more formal, less chatty style and the detail painting an accurate picture for readers.

ASSESSMENT

5. Expand it

Objective

To use expanded noun phrases to convey information.

What you need

Copies of *Varjak Paw*, interactive activity 'Meet the characters', notebooks.

What to do

- Write this sentence on the board: 'Varjak Paw is a cat.' Ask: *What sort of cat? What would help make the sentence more informative/interesting?* (detail) Underline 'Varjak Paw' and 'cat' and ask: *What parts of speech are they?* (proper noun – a name, so capitalised; a common noun) Remind children that a phrase is a group of words working together, but without a verb. Phrases add detail to other words. Noun phrases add detail to nouns to make them more specific.

- Invite words to describe Varjak, and demonstrate how to expand a noun: 'Varjak Paw is a Mesopotamian Blue cat.' Directly below, add another sentence: 'Varjak Paw is a pedigree, Mesopotamian Blue cat.' Then, 'Varjak Paw is a pure-bred, pedigree, Mesopotamian Blue cat.'

- Open interactive activity 'Meet the characters' and match the nouns to a suitable noun phrase.

- Ask children to design a 'missing' poster for four of the story's cats by dividing a page of their notebooks into four squares. They should describe each chosen cat using expanded noun phrases, for you to assess how well they have mastered them.

Differentiation

Support: Allow the children to repeat the interactive activity until they feel confident.
Extension: Encourage children to design a cat survey using expanded noun phrases to describe all the cats in the story, then conduct a poll to find out who liked which cat best.

6. Error alert!

Objective

To evaluate and edit their own writing.

What you need

Printable page 'Spot the errors', interactive activity 'Fix it', notebooks, dictionaries.

What to do

- Revise the importance of editing work to ensure it looks good and makes sense. Sloppy, inaccurate writing makes a poor impression and even stops the reader understanding properly. Ask: *What type of mistakes can easily occur when you write?* (for example: spelling, sentence construction, tense, punctuation, layout, register)

- Open the interactive activity 'Fix it' and let the children practise correcting the sentences. Each sentence has a specific error that relates to spelling, grammar or punctuation.

- Hand out printable pages 'Spot the errors'. Ask volunteers to read different sections of the text. Ask: *Was it difficult or easy to read aloud?* (Most readers will find it difficult because of the lack of punctuation and incorrect grammar, as well as the spelling errors. It is also makes it hard to read with expression.)

- Using the printable pages, ask children to identify the errors and classify them. It contains three of each type of error so the children can use this as a guide. It will also help you assess them. In their notebooks, the children can rewrite the text without errors.

Differentiation

Support: Go through the printable pages and discuss the errors before letting the children sort the errors with a partner.
Extension: Invite children to plan and write a paragraph with at least five deliberate errors for a partner to correct.

Read and understand

- Read Chapter 11 of *Varjak Paw* and answer the questions below.

1. Where were the cats having their conversation?

   _____

2. Is the dialogue formal or informal? Why?

   _____

3. Why did Holly call Varjak 'Poor Jack'?

   _____

4. Explain the expression 'Have a heart.'

   _____

5. Find a phrase in the text that means 'she's not as dangerous as she seems'.

   _____

6. Varjak used words that were unfamiliar to the other cats. Name two and explain why they were unfamiliar.

   _____

   _____

7. What do you think happened to Luka?

   _____

   _____

8. Identify the prefix and suffix in the word 'unapproachable'. What does 'unapproachable' mean?

   _____

   _____

9. How did Varjak feel when Holly and Tam laughed at him?

   _____

10. Why did Holly say 'friends are not worth having'?

   _____

SCHOLASTIC

Available in this series:

978-1407-16066-5

978-1407-16053-5

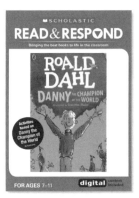

978-1407-16054-2

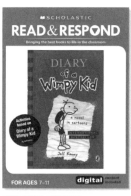

978-1407-16055-9

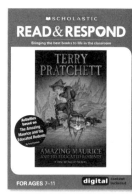

978-1407-16056-6

978-1407-16057-3

978-1407-16058-0

978-1407-16059-7

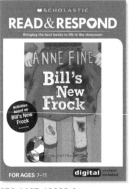

978-1407-16060-3

978-1407-16061-0

978-1407-16062-7

978-1407-16063-4

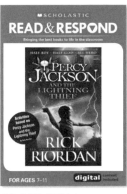

978-1407-16064-1

978-1407-16065-8

978-1407-16052-8

978-1407-16067-2

978-1407-16068-9

978-1407-16069-6

978-1407-16070-2

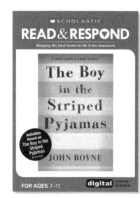

978-1407-16071-9

To find out more, call: 0845 6039091
or visit our website www.scholastic.co.uk/readandrespond